MARRIAGE NOTICES

IN

The South-Carolina and American General Gazette

FROM MAY 30, 1766, TO FEBRUARY 28, 1781
AND IN ITS SUCCESSOR

The Royal Gazette

(1781-1782)

Compiled and Edited by A. S. SALLEY, JR.,
Secretary of the Historical Commission of South Carolina

From the files in the library of the Charleston Library Society,
Charleston, S. C.

CLEAR~
FIELD

Originally Published
Columbia, South Carolina
1914

Reprinted
Genealogical Publishing Co., Inc.
Baltimore, 1976

Reprinted for Clearfield Company Inc. by
Genealogical Publishing Co. Inc.
Baltimore, MD 1990

Library of Congress Catalogue Card Number 76-16888
International Standard Book Number 0-8063-0726-9

Reprinted from a volume in
The North Carolina State Library
Raleigh, North Carolina

Made in the United States of America

INTRODUCTION

On Wednesday, November 22, 1758, Robert Wells began the publication in Charles Town of *The South-Carolina weekly Gazette*. With the issue for April 4, 1764, its name was changed to *The South-Carolina and American General Gazette*. The writer knows of but one paper now in existence between the first issue and the change of its name. That is possessed by Mrs. Charlotte D. Garriss, of Columbia, and is No. 12, Wednesday, February 7, 1759.

The South-Carolina Gazette of Monday, October 8, 1764, contains, under the date line "Charles-Town, *October* 1. 1764", "A short view of domestic occurrences, &c. since the discontinuance of this Gazette, from the 31st of March last" in which the following account is given of the change of the name of *The South-Carolina weekly Gazette* to *The South-Carolina and American General Gazette:*

April 4th, The paper hitherto called the *South-Carolina weekly Gazette*, appeared under the new and pompous title of "THE SOUTH-CAROLINA AND AMERICAN *GENERAL* GAZETTE," the *king's arms* at the head of it was displaced, to introduce a *new* cut; and the public was advertised, that *that* paper "*was circulated* IN ALL *the provinces of South-Carolina, North-* "*Carolina Georgia, East-Florida and West Florida, and sent to every place* "*of note on the British American continent and to all the islands, also to* "*Great-Britain and other parts of Europe, so that advertisements published* "*in it had a very general as well as speady circulation,*" &c.

The Charleston Library Society possesses a supplement to the issue for Wednesday, April 18, 1764, but its files begin regularly with the issue for Friday, May 30, 1766, being No. 395.

The following issues prior to 1772 are lacking in the Charleston Library Society's file:

Friday, June 27, 1766, No. 399.
Friday, August 29, 1766, No. 408.
Friday, December 4, 1767, No. 473.
Friday, April 1, 1768, No. 490.
Wednesday, December 20, 1769, No. 583.
Wednesday, December 27, 1769, No. 584.
Wednesday, January 3, 1770, No. 585.

Wednesday, January 10, 1770, No. 586.
Wednesday, January 17, 1770, No. 587.
Wednesday, January 24, 1770, No. 588.
Wednesday, July 31, 1771, No. 667.
Tuesday, December 10, 1771, No. 686.

From April 23, 1772, to April 22, 1774, the Library's file contains but a few scattering numbers, or parts of numbers, as follows:
Four pages (195-198) of Monday, August 10, 1772.
Four pages of Monday, September 28, 1772.
Monday, October 5, 1772.
Four pages (249-252) of Monday, October 19, 1772.
Thursday, October 22, 1772.
Two pages of Monday, November 2, 1772.
Four pages (69-72) of Monday, March 23, 1773.

From April 22, 1774, to May 31, 1776, the Library's file lacks the following issues:
Friday, February 3, 1775, No. 855.
Friday, June 23, 1775, No. 876.
Friday, October 27, 1775, No. 895.
Friday, November 3, 1775, No. 896.
Friday, November 10, 1775, No. 897.
Friday, November 17, 1775, No. 898.
Two pages (251-252) of Friday, December 22, 1775, No. 902.
Friday, January 5, 1776, No. 903.
Two pages (31-32) of Wednesday, March 20, 1776, No. 912.

After the issue for Friday, May 31, 1776, of which there are two copies in the Library's file, no paper was issued until Friday, August 2, 1776. From the latter date to April 30, 1779, the following issues are lacking in the Library's file:
Wednesday, August 28, to Wednesday, September 11, 1776, Nos. 924 and 925.
Thursday, October 24, 1776.
Thursday, November 14, 1776, No. 931.
Thursday, December 5, 1776, No. 934.
Two pages of Thursday, January 23, 1777, No. 940.
Thursday, March 6, 1777, No. 946.
Thursday, March 27, 1777, No. 949.

Two pages of Thursday, May 22, 1777, No. 958.
Two pages of Thursday, June 26, 1777, No. 964.
Thursday, December 4, 1777, No. 987.
Thursday, December 18, 1777, No. 989.
Thursday, April 9, 1778, No. 1003.
Two pages of Thursday, June 4, 1778, No. 1012.
Thursday, June 25, 1778, No. 1016.
Two pages of Thursday, October 29, 1778, No. 1034.
Two pages of Thursday, November 26, 1778, No. 1038.
Thursday, January 7, 1779, No. 1044.
Thursday, March 11, 1779, No. 1052.
Friday, April 2, 1779, No. 1055.

After the issue for Friday, April 30, 1779, no paper was issued until Saturday, May 29, 1779, on account of Prévost's invasion of South Carolina. Between the latter date and March 1, 1781, the following papers are lacking in the Library's file:
Saturday, June 5, to Friday, July 9, 1779, Nos. 1063-1065.
Friday, July 23, 1779, No. 1067.
Friday, August 6, 1779, No. 1069.
Friday, November 5, 1779, No. 1081.
Friday, November 12, 1779, No. 1082.
Friday, November 26, 1779, No. 1084.
Friday, December 24, 1779, to July 19, 1780, Nos. 1086-1091.
August 2, to September 13, 1780, Nos. 1093-1099.
September 27, to October 25, 1780, Nos. 1101-1109.

From this time on the paper was issued twice a week, Wednesday and Saturday. The following numbers are lacking in the Library's file:
November 8, and 11, 1780, Nos. 1112 and 1113.
November 18-December 2, 1780, Nos. 1115-1119.
Saturday, November 9, 1780, No. 1121.
Saturday, January 6, 1781, No. 1129.
Saturday, January 20, 1781, No. 1133.
Saturday, January 27, 1781, No. 1135.
Saturday, February 3, 1781, No. 1137.

In the issue for Wednesday, February 21, 1781, the following announcement appeared:

His Majesty having been pleased to appoint Robert Wells and Son his Printers in South Carolina; this Paper will be published, after the first of next Month, under the Title of THE ROYAL GAZETTE, which it shall be the constant Study of the EDITORS to render worthy of the Publick Favour. ☞It is requested that those in Arrears for this Paper, will immediately discharge the same.

No. 1. of Volume I. of *The Royal Gazette* appeared March 3, 1781, and its publication ceased some time prior to the British evacuation of Charles Town in December, 1782.

THE SOUTH-CAROLINA AND AMERICAN GENERAL GAZETTE.

MARRIED.] In Charlestown, July 7th. Captain Alexander Gillon, of the brigantine Free-Mason, to Mrs. Mary Cripps, widow of Mr. William Cripps. (Friday, July 11, 1766.)

MARRIED.] In Charlestown, Sept. 9th. Mr. Alexander Michie, Merchant, to Miss Henrietta Carrol. (Friday, Sept. 12, 1766.)

MARRIED.] Sept. 7th. Thomas Fuller, Esq; to Mrs. Elizabeth Miles, relict of Mr. Edward Miles. (Friday, September 19, 1766.)

MARRIED.] October 4. Mr. Alexander Chisolme, jun. to Miss Christiana Chisolme, Daughter of Mr. Alexander Chisolme.— Captain John Moncreiff, of the Brigantine Smyth, to Mary Fley.—October 9th. Mr. Samuel Prioleau, jun. to Miss Katherine Cordes, Daughter of John Cordes, Esq; deceased. (Friday, October 10, 1766.)

MARRIED.] Mr. Francis Clayton, of North-Carolina, merchant, to Miss Mary Colcock, daughter of the deceased John Colcock, Esq; (Friday, November 21, 1766.)

MARRIED.] Lately at Philadelphia, Mr. Isaac Lessesne, jun. of this place, merchant, to Miss Hannah Noarth, daughter of Captain George Noarth, of Philadelphia. (Friday, November 28, 1766.)

MARRIED.] Benjamin Guerard, Esq; to Miss Sarah Middleton, Daughter of Col. Thomas Middleton, Esq;—John Matthewes, jun. Esq; to Miss Mary Wragg, Daughter of William Wragg, Esq; (Friday, December 5, 1766.)

MARRIED.] Honourable Thomas Skottowe, Esq; to Miss Lucia Bellinger, daughter of Edmond Bellinger, Esq; Mr. Thomas Lind, to Miss Catharine Smith.—In Georgia, Mr. George Baillie, to Miss Jourdina Crooke. (Monday, December 29, 1766.)

MARRIED.] Mr. Andrew Cunningham, merchant, to Mrs. Margaret Cochran, widow of Doctor John Cochran. (Friday, January 9, 1767.)

MARRIED.] Mr. William Somersall, of St. Christophers, to Miss Sally Legaré, daughter of Mr. Thomas Legaré, of this town. (Friday, January 16, 1767.)

On Tuesday last, the Honourable ROBERT CATHERWOOD, Esq; of St. Augustine, was married to Miss Jenny Chads, lately arrived here from England, sister of Captain Chads of his Majesty's Navy. (Friday, February 13, 1767.)

MARRIED.] Feb. 15th. Mr. Robert Swainston, of Watboo, to Miss Deborah Sabb.—19th. Mr. John Lord, to Miss Broun, daughter of Robert Broun, Esq; deceased.—22d. John Matthewes, Esq; to Miss Nancy Harvey, daughter of Mr. John Harvey.—Mr. Thomas Netherclift, of Georgia, merchant, to Miss Nancy Macqueen, daughter of John Macqueen, Esq; deceased. (Friday, February 27, 1767.)

MARRIED.] James Hasell, junior, Esq; of North-Carolina, to Miss Susanna Foissin.—Dr. Barnet Wait to Mrs. Martha Urquahart. (Friday, March 6, 1767.)

MARRIED] March 8th, "Anthony la Motte, Esq; the only son of Messire René Douin de la Motte, one of the King of France's counsellors, and chief secretary in the ministry, to Miss Dorcas Randall, the only daughter to the Honourable William Randall, Esq; surveyour general of his Majesty's customs in the southern district in America, and accomplished young lady."—Mr. William Cattel to Miss Sabina Lynch, daughter of Thomas Lynch, Esq;—March 10th, John Gordon, Esq; to Miss Kitty Smith, daughter of the Honourable William Smith, Esq; a member of his Majesty's council in New-York. (Friday, March 13, 1767.)

MARRIED] John Huger, Esq; to Miss Charlotte Motte, daughter of Jacob Motte, Esq; Publick Treasurer of this province.—Mr. Edward Oats to Miss Elisabeth Walker, niece of Captain Thomas Walker deceased. (Friday, March 20, 1767.)

MARRIED] Mr. Thomas Hartley to Mrs. Mary Hiatt, widow of Mr. Anthony Hiatt. (Friday, April 3, 1767.)

MARRIED.] At Savannah, Captain Thomas Savage, of this town, to Miss Polly Butler, only daughter of the deceased William Butler, Esq.—In Charlestown, Dr. John Delahowe to Mrs. Anne Boyd, widow of Captain Robert Boyd. (Friday, May 1, 1767.)

MARRIED] At Bath in England. William Haggat, Esq; to Miss Elizabeth Walter, daughter of the deceased Colonel Walter of this province.—At New York. Ralph Izard, of this province, Esq; to Miss Alice DeLancey, daughter of Peter DeLancey, Esq; of West-Chester. (Friday, June 5, 1767.)

MARRIED] Mr. Francis Rose, to Miss Betsey Lining, daughter of the deceased Dr. John Lining. (Friday, July 3, 1767.)

MARRIED] Mr. James Graham, merchant, to Miss Sally Stuart, daughter of the Honourable John Stuart, Esq. (Friday, July 17, 1767.)

MARRIED.] Benjamin Huger, Esq; to Miss Polly Golightly, daughter of Culcheth Golightly, Esq; deceased. (Friday, July 24, 1767.)

MARRIED.] Mr. Francis Varambaut, to Mrs. Anne Lataw.—In Georgia, John Milledge, Esq; to Mrs. Anne Rasberry. (Friday, July 31, 1767.)

MARRIED] Dr. John Anderson to Mrs. Anne Gordon, widow of the Revd. Charles Gordon.—Mr. Daniel Price to Miss Eleanor Jones, sister of Mr. Edward Jones. (Friday, August 7, 1767.)

MARRIED] Mr. Edward Thomas, to Miss Anne Gibbes, daughter of Mr. William Gibbes.—Mr. Andrew Rutledge, to Miss Elizabeth Gadsden, daughter of Christopher Gadsden, Esq; (Friday, October 2, 1767.)

MARRIED] Mr. John Baker, merchant, to Miss Amy Legarè, daughter of Mr. Thomas Legarè. (Friday, October 16, 1767.)

MARRIED,] Honourable John Burn, Esq; to Mrs. Anne Baron, widow of Mr. Alexander Baron.—Mr. James Stanyarne, to Mrs. Henrietta Raven, widow of Mr. William Raven.—Mr. Alexander Alexander, to Miss Rachel Anderson.—Mr. David Guerard, to Miss Judith de St. Julien. (Friday, October 30, 1767.)

MARRIED] Mr. Peter Valton, to Miss Betsey Timothy, daughter of Mr. Peter Timothy. (Friday, November 6, 1767.)

MARRIED.] Mr. John MacCall, jun. to Miss Charlotte Glen, daughter of Mr. William Glen. (Friday, November, 13, 1767.)

MARRIED.] Mr. Edward Griffith, merchant, to Miss Patty Miles, daughter of Mr. Thomas Miles, deceased.—Mr. George Blakie to Mrs. Elisabeth Roffe, widow of Mr. John Roffe. (Friday, November 27, 1767.)

MARRIED] Mr. George Thomson, merchant, to Miss Jeanie Yorston, a young lady lately arrived here from Edinburgh. (Friday, December 18, 1767.)

MARRIED.] Daniel Horry Esq; to Miss Harriett Pinckney, Daughter of the honourable Charles Pinckney, Esq; a Member of his Majesty's Council and Chief Justice of this Province, deceased. —Mr. Charles Shepheard, Merchant, to Miss Elizabeth Radcliffe, Daughter of Mr. Thomas Radcliffe.—Mr. David Dott, Merchant, to Miss Sarah Baker, of St. Andrew's Parish. (Friday, February 19, 1768.)

MARRIED.] The Reverend Mr. John Thomas, Minister of the Independent or New England Meeting in this Town, to Miss Mary Lamboll, the only Child of Thomas Lamboll, Esq; (Friday, February 26, 1768.)

MARRIED.] Mr. Roger Smith, Merchant, to Miss Mary Rutledge, Daughter of the deceased Dr. John Rutledge, Esq; (Friday, April 8, 1768.)

MARRIED.] William Brisbane, Esq; to Miss Eunace Stevens, Daughter of the Reverend Mr. Stevens. (Friday, April 15, 1768.)

MARRIED] Mr. Nathaniel Fuller, to Miss Nancy Fuller, Daughter of Thomas Fuller, Esq. (Friday, April 22, 1768.)

MARRIED] Mr. Thomas Osborn, of Jacksonburgh, to Mrs. Catharine Spry, Widow of Mr. Joseph Spry. (Friday, April 29, 1768.)

MARRIED.] Reverend Mr. John Tonge, Rector of St. Paul's, to Miss Susanna Perry, Daughter of Edward Perry, Esq. (Friday, September 9, 1768.)

MARRIED] Mr. Robert Dillon, to Miss Christiana Chiffelle, daughter of the Rev. Mr. Chiffelle, rector of St. Peter's, Purrysburgh, deceased. (Friday, October 14, 1768.)

MARRIED] Mr. Thomas Doughty to Miss Mary Legaré, Daughter of Mr. Daniel Legaré, sen.—Mr. William Richardson to Miss Anne Guignard, Daughter of Mr. Gabriel Guignard, deceased. (Friday, October 21, 1768.)

MARRIED] John Colcock, Esq; to Miss Millicent Jones. (Friday, November 4, 1768.)

MARRIED.] Mr. James Christie to Miss Hephzibah Rose.—Mr. Richard Waring to Miss Nancy Branford. (Friday, November 25, 1768.)

MARRIED.] In Charlestown, Mr. John Scott, junr. to Miss Sarah Peronneau.—On John's Island, Mr. Thomas Ladson to Miss Mary Cole; Mr. Nathaniel Barnwell to Miss Elizabeth Waight.—At Dorchester, Mr. Isaac Droze to Miss Mary Elisabeth Dowse. (Monday, December 19, 1768.)

MARRIED] Capt. Richard Todd, to Miss Elisabeth Winborn, only child of the late Mr. Samuel Winborn.—Mr. John Webb, to Miss Mary Doughty, daughter of the late Mr. Thomas Doughty. (Monday, January 9, 1769.)

MARRIED] William Skirving, Esq; to Miss Anne Hutchinson, daughter of Thomas Hutchinson, Esq.—Mr. Benjamin Merchant, to Miss Frances Timothy, daughter of Mr. Peter Timothy. (Monday, January 23, 1769.)

MARRIED.] Stephen Drayton, Esq; to Miss Elizabeth Waring. (Monday, January 30, 1769.)

MARRIED.] On Sunday last, William Wragg, Esq; to Miss Henrietta Wragg, daughter of the Honourable Joseph Wragg, Esq; deceased. (Monday, February 6, 1769.)

MARRIED.] John Savage, Esq; to Miss Anne Gaillard.[1]—Capt. George Higgins, of the Snow Portland, to Miss Elisabeth Colles. (Monday, February 13, 1769.)

They write from Georgia, that Basil Cowper, esq; was married the 15th inst. to the amiable Miss Polly Smith, daughter of John Smith, esq. (Monday, February 27, 1769.)

MARRIED] Mr. Arnout Schermerhorn, to Miss Polly Mackay, daughter of the late deceased Capt. John Mackay. Mr. William Lee, to Miss Nancy Theus, daughter of Mr. Jeremiah Theus. (Monday, March 6, 1769.)

MARRIED] James Skirving, Esq; to Mrs. Charlotte Matthews, widow of James Matthews, Esq. (Monday, March 20, 1769.)

MARRIED.] Mr. William Telfair, of Georgia, Merchant, to Miss Elisabeth Bellinger, daughter of Edmond Bellinger, Esq.—Roger Pinckney, Esq; to Mrs. Susanna Hume, widow of Robert Hume, Esq.—Mr. James Harvey, Merchant, to Miss Mary Gibbes, daughter of Culcheth Gibbes, Esq.—Mr. Thomas Walter, Merchant, to Miss Anne Lessesne, daughter of Mr. Isaac Lessesne. (Monday, March 27, 1769.)

MARRIED.] John Mackenzie, Esq; to Miss Sally Smith, daughter of Thomas Smith, jun. Esq.—Mr. James Cassels, of Georgetown,. to Miss Nancy[2] Mann, daughter of the late Dr. Mann. (Monday, April 3, 1769.)

MARRIED.] ALEXANDER WRIGHT, Esq; son of his Excellency James Wright, Esq; Governour in chief, &c. of his Majesty's Province of Georgia, to Miss ELIZABETH IZARD, Daughter of John Izard, Esq; deceased. (Monday, April 10, 1769.)

---

[1] "The Account, in a former Paper, of the Marriage of John Savage, Esq; of Ninety Six to Miss Gaillard is not true."—Monday, April 17, 1769.

[2] "Mr. James Cassels of Georgetown, is married to Miss Sukey (not Miss Nancy) Mann."—Monday, April 17, 1769.

MARRIED] Dr. GEORGE HAIG, to Miss SUSANNA MACKEWN, Daughter of Robert Mackewn, Esq; deceased. (Monday, May 1, 1769.)

MARRIED.] Mr. John Perkins to Miss Sarah Cozzens of Georgia. (Monday, May 8, 1769.)

MARRIED.] Charles Dudley, Esq; (late of this Province) Collector of his Majesty's Customs at Rhode-Island, to Miss Crook, Daughter of Robert Crook, Esq;—Mr. William Johnson, to Miss Nightingall, Daughter of Mr. Thomas Nightingall. (Monday, May 15, 1769.)

MARRIED] Paul Trapier, Esq; of Georgetown, to Mrs. Waties, Widow of John Waties, Esq.—Mr. Henry Webster, of Ponpon, to the Widow Ford of Willtown—Dr. William Remington, to Miss Anne Iten—Dr. Alexander Fitzgerald of Cape Fear, to the Widow Beatty of Ponpon. (Monday, May 29, 1769.)

MARRIED] Mr. THOMAS CORBETT, Merchant, to Miss MARGARET HARLESTON, Daughter of the late John Harleston, Esq. (Monday, June 12, 1769.)

MARRIED] Capt. Charles-Augustus Steward of his Majesty's 21st Regiment, to Miss Dolly Powell, Daughter of George-Gabriel Powell, Esq. (Tuesday, June 20, 1769.)

MARRIED.] Lately at St. Augustine, Lieut. Frederick Muncaster, of the Royal Regiment of Artillery, to Miss DeBrahm, Daughter of William-Gerhard DeBrahm, Esq; Surveyor-General of the Southern District of North-America. (Monday, July 10, 1769.)

MARRIED.] Mr. John Bull, to Miss Sarah Phillips, Sister of James Phillips, Esq. (Monday, July 17, 1769.)

MARRIED] Mr. Godin Guerard to Miss Nancy Matthews, Daughter of the deceased John Matthews, Esq. (Wednesday, August 30, 1769.)

MARRIED.] Dr. Archibald MacNeill, to Miss Elisabeth Postell, Daughter of Elijah Postell, Esq.—Mr. Richard Wayne, Merchant, to Miss Elisabeth Clifford, Daughter of the late Mr. Thomas Clifford. (Monday, September 18, 1769.)

14

MARRIED.] Mr. John Brailsford, to Miss Elisabeth Muncreef, Daughter of Mr. Richard Muncreef.—Mr. George Ancrum, to Miss Catharine Porcher, Daughter of Isaac Porcher, Esq.—Mr. Eli Kershaw, to Miss Mary Cantey, Daughter of John Cantey, Esq. (Monday, December 4, 1769.)

MARRIED.] Mr. Elias Jaudon, to Miss Mary Dickson, Daughter of the deceased Capt. Thomas Dickson. (Wednesday, February 14, 1770.)

MARRIED.] Mr. William Doughty, Merchant, to Miss Rachel Porcher, Daughter of Isaac Porcher, Esq. (Friday, February 23, 1770.)

MARRIED.] Mr. Benjamin Matthews, Merchant, to Miss Sally Sams, Daughter of the deceased Capt. Sams. Mr. Thomas Screven, to Miss Nelly Hart, Daughter of the reverend Oliver Hart. (Friday, March 16, 1770.)

MARRIED.] John Simpson, Esq; of Georgia, to Miss Elizabeth Dale, Daughter of the late —— Dale, Esq; of North-Carolina. (Friday, March 30, 1770.)

MARRIED.] Mr. William Glen, jun. Merchant, to Miss Martha Miller, Daughter of Stephen Miller, Esq. (Friday, April 13, 1770.)

MARRIED.] Thomas Hayward, Esq; Captain of his Majesty's Ship Martin, to Miss Anne Sinclair, Daughter of the late Mr. John Sinclair. (Friday, April 27, 1770.)

MARRIED.] James Carson, Esq; to Mrs. Anne Stuart, Widow of Francis Stuart, Esq. (Friday, May 4, 1770.)

MARRIED.] Mr. Brian Cape, Merchant, to Mrs. Mary Hetherington, Widow of Mr. John Hetherington, and Daughter of Stephen Miller, Esq.—Mr. John Robert, of Indian-Land, to Miss Elizabeth Dixon, Daughter of the deceased Capt. Thomas Dixon, of James-Island.—In Georgia, James Hume, Esq; to Miss Mary Tannatt, Daughter of the late Edmund Tannatt, Esq. (Friday, May 11, 1770.)

MARRIED.] Mr. David Gillespie, A. B. to Mrs. Mary Rogers, Widow of Capt. James Rogers.—Capt. Edward Darrell, to Miss Anne Smith, Daughter of the Reverend Josiah Smith.—Mr. Robert Rose, to Miss Rebecca Rivers, Daughter of the deceased Mr. John Rivers. (Wednesday, May 23, 1770.)

MARRIED.] Mr. Thomas Rose, to Miss Mary-Anne Clarke Saunders, Daughter of the deceased Joshua Saunders, Esq; of St. Bartholomew's Parish. (Wednesday, May 30, 1770.)

MARRIED.] Mr. Ulysses Macpherson, to Miss Sarah Laird, only Child of the late Mr. John Laird.—Mr. Samuel Hopkins, to Mrs. Frances Dandridge, Widow of Mr. William Dandridge.—Mr. Mark Morris, to Miss Margaret Tew.—Mr. John Chesnut, to Miss Sarah Cantey. (Friday, June 15, 1770.)

MARRIED] Mr. Charles Johnston, Merchant, to Miss Mary Mackenzie, only Child of Mr. Robert Mackenzie, Merchant. (Friday, June 22, 1770.)

MARRIED.] Mr. Jonathan Sarrazin, to Mrs. Sarah Prioleau, Widow of Elijah Prioleau, Esq.—Mr. George Flagg, to Miss Anderson, daughter of Mr. John Anderson. (Wednesday, July 25, 1770.)

MARRIED.] Mr. William Air, to Miss Mary Stevenson, Daughter of the deceased Capt. Charles Stevenson. Mr. Thomas Jervey, to Miss Grace Hall, Daughter of the late Mr. William Hall. (Friday, August 3, 1770.)

MARRIED.] Mr. William Hopkins, to Miss Elisabeth Welch. (Monday, August 20, 1770.)

MARRIED.] John Waring, Esq; to Mrs. Charlotte Williamson, Widow of Champernown Williamson, Esq. (Monday, September, 17, 1770.)

MARRIED.] Stephen Miller, Esq; to Miss Mary Roche, Daughter of the deceased Francis Roche, Esq. David Guerard, Esq; to Miss Martha Barnwell, Daughter of John Barnwell, Esq—Mr. James Lessley, to Mrs. Mary Stokes, Widow of the Rev. Mr. Stokes. (Monday, September 24, 1770.)

MARRIED.] Peter Delancey, Esq; Post-Master General of the Southern District of North-America, to Miss Elisabeth Beresford, Daughter of Richard Beresford, Esq. (Wednesday, October 3, 1770.)

MARRIED.] Dr. James-Weems Moore, to Miss Susannah Jones, Daughter of the deceased Mr. Charles Jones. (Tuesday, October 9, 1770.)

Sir William Draper, Knight of the Bath, &c. &c. was lately married at New-York to Miss Sukey Delancey, Daughter of Oliver Delancey, Esq; and was to sail, about this Time, with his new-married Lady for London, in the Ship Dutchess of Gordon. (Tuesday, October 23, 1770.)

MARRIED] Mr. John Wilkie, to Mrs. Jane Hext, Widow of Mr. Alexander Hext. (Wednesday, October 31, 1770.)

"A few days ago was married, in St. Bartholomew's-Parish, Mr. JAMES JORDAN, to Miss SUSANNAH CHRISTY, an agreeable young Lady, with a handsome Fortune." (Tuesday, November 6, 1770.)

MARRIED.] Elias Horry, jun. Esq; to Miss Elisabeth Branford, eldest Daughter of the deceased William Branford, Esq.—Alexander Mazyck, Esq; to Miss Charlotte Broughton, Daughter of Nathaniel Broughton, Esq.—Mr. Edward Kirk, of New-Providence, to Miss Charlotte Bennet. (Tuesday, November 20, 1770.)

MARRIED.] Mr. Andrew Lord, Merchant, to Mrs. Gadsden, Widow of Thomas Gadsden, Esq. (Tuesday, November 27, 1770.)

MARRIED.] Major Pierce Butler, of the 29th Regiment, to Miss Polly Middleton, Daughter of the deceased Colonel Thomas Middleton—Mr. John Brewton, Merchant, to Miss Polly Weyman, Daughter of Mr. Edward Weyman. (Monday, January 14, 1771.)

MARRIED.] Robert Williams, jun Esq; to Miss Anne Roper, eldest Daughter of William Roper Esq. (Tuesday, February 19, 1771.)

MARRIED.] Mr. John Potter, to Miss Sarah Hinds, Daughter of Mr. Patrick Hinds. (Wednesday, February 27, 1771.)

MARRIED.] Mr. Arnoldus Vanderhorst, to Miss Elizabeth Raven, only Child of the deceased William Raven, Esq. (Tuesday, March 12, 1771.)

MARRIED. John Nevin, Esq; to Miss Nancy Baker. (Tuesday, March 26, 1771.)

MARRIED. Dr. Peter Spence, to Miss Frances Brown, Daughter of Joseph Brown, Esq.—Mr. Nathan Tart, to Miss Frances Garden, Daughter of the Rev. Alexander Garden, Rector of St. Thomas's—Mr. William Scott, jun to Miss Elizabeth Legaré, Daughter of Mr. Daniel Legaré, Sen. (Wednesday, April 10, 1771.)

MARRIED. Isaac Chanler, M. D. to Miss Sarah White. (Wednesday, April 17, 1771.)

MARRIED. William Roper, jun. Esq; to Miss Hannah Dart, Daughter of Benjamin Dart, Esq. (Monday, May 6, 1771.)

MARRIED. Mr. Daniel Heyward, jun. to Miss Margaret Heyward.—Mr. Thomas Bull, to Miss Sarah Simpson. (Monday, May 13, 1771.)

MARRIAGES. Mr. John Lining, to Miss Mary Rivers—Mr. Henry Crouch, to Miss Josepha Watson. (Monday, June 10, 1771.)

MARRIAGE. Mr. John Fraser, to Miss Polly Stobo, Daughter of James Stobo, Esq. (Monday, July 1, 1771.)

MARRIAGES. Dr Benjamin Willply, to Miss Sally Mac Gaw.—Col. Christopher Rowe, to Mrs. Chevillette, Widow of Col. John Chevillette. (Monday, July 8, 1771.)

MARRIAGE. Benjamin Wigfall, Esq; to Miss Martha Dutarque. (Tuesday, August 6, 1771.)

MARRIAGES. Daniel Heyward, sen. Esq; to Miss Elizabeth Simons, Daughter of Benjamin Simons, sen. Esq. Mr. John Inrie to Mrs. Elisabeth Russel, Widow of Mr. Alexander Russel. —At Purysburg August 27th, 1771, Mr. Acquilla Miles, to Mrs.[1] (Tuesday, September 10, 1771.)

MARRIAGES. Mr. Edward Simons, to Miss Lydia Ball—Mr. William Swallow, to Miss Sarah Prince. (Monday, October 28, 1771.)

MARRIAGE. Mr. Robert Porteous, of Beaufort, Merchant, to Miss Anne Wigg, of the same Place, Daughter of the late Col. Wigg. (Monday, November 18, 1771.)

MARRIAGES. Paul Trapier, jun. Esq; to Miss Elisabeth Foissin, Daughter of the late Elias Foissin, Esq. Mr. Edward Jermaine, to Miss Sarah Cahusac.—Mr. John Miot, to Miss Frances Harden. (Monday, November 25, 1771.)

MARRIAGE. Mr. James Wakefield, Merchant, to Miss Sally Cannon, Daughter of Mr. Daniel Cannon. (Tuesday, December 3, 1771.)

MARRIAGES. Mr. William Wilson, Merchant, to Miss Polly Harvey, Daughter of William Harvey, Esq. Capt. Benjamin Darrell, to Mrs. Kezia Boone, Widow of the late Mr. Samuel Boone. (Monday, January 6, 1772—Supplement.)

MARRIAGE. Mr. William Hort to Miss Alice Gibbes, Daughter of Mr. Robert Gibbes, deceased. (Monday, January 13, 1772.)

MARRIAGE. Peter Fayssoux, M. D. to Miss Sarah Wilson, Daughter of Algernon Wilson, Esq. (Thursday, February 6, 1772.)

MARRIAGE. Mr. John Screven, of James Island, to Miss Patience Holmes, youngest Daughter of Mr. John Holmes, of John's Island. (Thursday, February 20, 1772.)

MARRIAGE. Mr. Robert Mackay of Augusta, to Mrs. Chilcott, late of Rhode-Island. (Tuesday, February 25, 1772.)

---

[1]Rest torn out.

MARRIAGE. Andrew Johnston Esq; to Miss Sarah-Elliott Mackewn, Daughter of the deceased Robert Mackewn Esq;. (Monday, March 2, 1772.)

MARRIAGES. Mr. James Ballandine, Merchant, to Miss Sally Buchanan.—Mr. Samuel Maverick, to Miss Lydia Turpin. (Monday, March 9, 1772.)

MARRIAGE. Robert Quash, junior, Esq; to Miss Constantia Hasell.[1] (Monday, March 30, 1772.)

MARRIAGE. Mr. Edward Gunter to Miss Martha Mellichamp. (Monday, April 6, 1772.)

MARRIAGE. In Georgia, John Simpson, Esq; of Sabine fields, to Miss Anne Mackenzie, Daughter of William Mackenzie Esq. (Monday, August 10, 1772.)

MARRIAGE. Richard Shubrick, Esq; to Miss Susannah Bulline, Daughter of Thomas Bulline, Esq; deceased. (Monday, October 5, 1772.)

MARRIAGES. Edmond Cossens, Esq; to Miss Jones. *"Beaufort,* April 10th, 1774. This day was married Nicholas Lechmere, Esq; to Miss Catharine Deveaux, Daughter of Andrew Deveaux, Esq; a Lady of an agreeable Person, and of a Disposition the most amiable and engaging." (Friday, April 22, 1774.)

MARRIAGE. Nicholas Eveleigh, Esq; to the amiable Miss Mary Shubrick, Daughter of Thomas Shubrick, Esq. (Friday, May 6, 1774.)

MARRIAGE. Mr. James Rantowle, to Miss Elisabeth Ives. (Friday, May 13, 1774.)

MARRIAGE. Revd. James Henderson, Minister at Edisto, to Mrs. Hannah Sands, Widow of Mr. James Sands, Merchant. (Friday, May 20, 1774.)

---

[1]"Robert Quash, junior, Esq; is not married to Miss Constantia Hasell."
—Monday, April 6, 1772.

MARRIAGE. Mr. Keating Simons, to Miss Sarah Lewis. (Friday, June 10, 1774.)

MARRIAGE. James Donnom, Esq; to Mrs. Jane Pepper, Widow of Daniel Pepper, jun. Esq. (Friday, June 17, 1774.)

MARRIAGES. Thomas-Tudor Tucker, M. D. to Miss Esther Evans, Daughter of George Evans, Esq. Mr. Charles Ramadge, to Mrs. Frances Swallow, Widow of Mr. Newman Swallow, Merchant. (Friday, July 8, 1774.)

MARRIAGE. Mr. Richard Lushington, Merchant, to Mrs. Ball, Widow of Mr. William Ball. (Friday, July 15, 1774.)

MARRIAGE. Mr. Benjamin Coachman, jun. to the amiable Miss Rebecca Singellton. (Friday, July 29, 1774.)

MARRIAGE. Thomas Ferguson, Esq; to Mrs. Elisabeth Rutledge, Widow of Mr. Andrew Rutledge, Merchant, and Daughter of Christopher Gadsden, Esq. (Friday, August 5, 1774.)

MARRIAGES. In Georgia, Nathaniel Hall, Esq; to Miss Anne Gibbons, Daughter of Joseph Gibbons, Esq; deceased.—In this Town, Mr. John Boomer, to Mrs. Elisabeth Cleator, Widow of Mr. John Cleator. (Friday, August 19, 1774.)

MARRIAGE. John Dutarque, Esq; to Miss Lydia Gaillard, Daughter of Theodore Gaillard, Esq. (Friday, August 26, 1774.)

MARRIAGE. At Saltketchers, Dr. Nathan Brownson, to Mrs. Elisabeth Martin, Widow of John Martin, Esq; late of Newport in Georgia. (Friday, September 2, 1774.)

MARRIAGE. Mr. Jeremiah Brower, Merchant, to Miss Christian Miller, Daughter of Stephen Miller, Esq. (Friday, September 9, 1774.)

MARRIAGES. Mr. Josiah Bonneau, Merchant, to Miss Susanna Eberson.—Mr. Patrick Murray, to Miss Oats, Daughter of Mr. Edward Oats.—In Georgia, Hon. Henry Yonge, Esq; to Miss Christiana Bulloch, Daughter of James Bulloch, Esq. (Friday, September 23, 1774.)

MARRIAGE. Mr. John Imrie, to Mrs. Margaret Esmand, Widow of Mr. George Esmand, late Printer in Barbados. (Friday, October 7, 1774.)

MARRIAGES. Mr. Joseph Atkinson, Merchant, to Miss Mary Burrows, Daughter of William Burrows, Esq. Mr. Thomas Rose, to Miss Mary Blake, Daughter of Capt. Edward Blake. (Friday, October 14, 1774.)

MARRIAGES. Thomas Middleton, Esq; to the amiable Miss Mary Gibbes, Daughter of Robert Gibbes, Esq.—Capt. John Sommers, to Miss Martha Perry, Daughter of Edward Perry, Esq; deceased. —Mr. Thomas Broughton, jun. to Miss Elisabeth Lessesne, Daughter of the late Mr. Isaac Lessesne.—Mr. Charles Cogdell, to Mrs. Jane Wilkie, Widow of Mr. John Wilkie.—Mr. Job Palmer, to Miss Sarah Morgan. (Friday, November 4, 1774.)

MARRIAGES. David Rhind, Esq; to Miss Elisabeth Cleiland, Daughter of the late Dr. John Cleiland.—Mr. William Webb, to Miss Margaret Doyley, Daughter of the late Daniel Doyley, Esq. (Friday, December 23, 1774.)

MARRIAGE. William Elliott, Esq; of Beaufort, to Mrs. Mary Cuthbert, Widow of James Cuthbert, Esq; late of Georgia. (Friday, January 6, 1775.)

MARRIAGES. Mr. Jacob Ion, to Miss Mary Ashby. Mr. George Heriot, Merchant in Georgetown, to Miss Sarah Tucker, Daughter of Capt. Thomas Tucker. William Allston, jun. Esq; to Miss Rachel Moore, Daughter of John Moore, Esq.—Capt. Isaac Burton, to Miss Anne Remington, Daughter of John Remington, Esq. (Friday, January 20, 1775.)

MARRIAGE. Richard Howley, Esq; to Mrs. Sarah Fuller. (Friday, January 27, 1775.)

MARRIAGES. David Ramsay, A. M. M. B. to Miss Sabina Ellis, Daughter of the deceased Mr. William Ellis, Merchant in this Town.—Mr. George John Fardo, to Miss Elizabeth Godfrey. (Friday, February 10, 1775.)

MARRIAGES. Mr. Daniel Hall, Merchant, to Miss Susanna Matthews, Daughter of the late William Matthews, Esq.—Mr. James Hampden Thomson, A. M. late Tutor in the College of New Jersey, to Miss Elisabeth-Martha Trezevant. (Friday, February 24, 1775.)

MARRIAGE. Rowland Rugely, Esq; to Miss Hamilton Dawson, Daughter of the Reverend Mr. Dawson, Rector of St. John's Parish, Colleton County, deceased. (Friday, March 17, 1775.)

MARRIAGE. Honourable John Drayton, Esq; to Miss Rebecca Perry, Daughter of Mr. Benjamin Perry, deceased.—Reverend James Latta, to Miss Sarah Wilson, Daughter of Mr. Hugh Wilson, deceased—Mr. Plowden Weston, Merchant, to Miss Mary Anne Mazyck, Daughter of Isaac Mazyck, Esq; deceased.—Mr. Daniel Holmes, to Miss Elisabeth Freer, Daughter of Mr. Solomon Freer. (Friday, March 24, 1775.)

MARRIAGE. Mr. John Bradwell, to Miss Elisabeth Lloyd, Daughter of the late Mr. William Lloyd. (Friday, March 31, 1775.)

MARRIAGES. Mr. Benjamin Webb to Miss Anne Doyley, daughter of the late Daniel Doyley, Esq.—Mr. Robert Muncreef to Miss Mary Dewar, Daughter of Mr. Charles Dewar. (Friday, April 7, 1775.)

MARRIAGES. Mr. Hext Prioleau to Miss Margaret Williams, an accomplished young Lady, Daughter of Robert Williams, jun. Esq. (Tuesday, April 18, 1775.)

MARRIAGES. Mr. John Bush, Merchant, to Mrs. Mary Miles, Widow of Mr. William Miles.—"In January last was married, at Port-Arlington in Ireland, Paul Mazyck, Esq; to Miss Hamon, only Daughter of the Rev. Dr. Hamon of the said Place; an amiable and most accomplished young Lady." (Friday, April 21, 1775.)

MARRIAGES. Mr. Edward Legge, of Ashley-Ferry, to Mrs. Waldren, Widow of Mr. Patrick Waldren. Mr. William Burt, to Miss Anne Jones. (Friday, May 5, 1775.)

MARRIAGES. Mr. John Cordes, to Miss Judith Banbury, Daughter of Mr. William Banbury.—Dr. William Clarkson, to Miss Anne Hutchinson. (Friday, May 12, 1775.)

MARRIAGES. Mr. Paul Porcher, jun. to Miss Jane Jackson.[1]—Mr. Samuel Eaton to Mrs. Providence Jenkins, Widow of the late Mr. Samuel Jenkins, of Edisto. Mr. Hamilton Stevenson to Miss J. Murray. (Friday, May 26, 1775.)

MARRIAGE. Mr. James Bentham, Merchant, to Miss Polly Hardy. (Friday, June 9, 1775.)

MARRIAGES. John-Raven Mathewes, Esq; to Miss Elisabeth Holmes, Daughter of Isaac Holmes, Esq; deceased.—John Frierson, Esq; to Miss Polly-Walne Davis, eldest Daughter of the Rev. Mr. William Davis, deceased. (Friday, June 16, 1775.)

MARRIAGE. John Glaze, Esq; to Mrs. Margaret McNeil, Widow of Dr. Archibald McNeil, deceased. (Friday, June 30, 1775.)

MARRIAGE. Mr. Samuel Jaudon to Miss Elisabeth Atkinson. (Friday, July 7, 1775.)

MARRIAGES. Benjamin Smith, Esq; to Miss Sarah Smith, Daughter of Mr. George Smith, Merchant.—Capt. Thomas Tucker to Mrs. Mary Flinn, Widow of the late Mr. William Flinn. Mr. Thomas Ellis to Miss Anne Glaze. (Friday, August 11, 1775.)

MARRIAGE. Mr. Charles Shepherd to Miss Elisabeth Gibbes, Daughter of William Gibbes, Esq. (Friday, September 1, 1775.)

MARRIAGE. Philotheos Chiffelle, Esq; to the amiable Miss Rebecca Hutchinson, Daughter of Thomas Hutchinson, Esq. (Friday, October 20, 1775.)

MARRIAGE. Mr. Jervis Henry Stevens, to Miss Elisabeth Davis, Daughter of the late Rev. Mr. John Davis, of St. Mark's Parish. (Friday, December 15, 1775.)

---

[1]"The Intimation in our last, of the Marriage of Mr. Paul Porcher, jun. to Miss Jane Jackson, was premature."—Friday, June 2, 1775.

MARRIAGE. Dr. James Clitherall, to Mrs. Elisabeth Smith, Widow of Thomas-Loughton Smith, Esq; deceased. (Friday, December 22, 1775.)

MARRIAGES. Major Barnard Elliott to Miss Susannah Smith, Daughter of Benjamin Smith, Esq; deceased. Colonel Isaac Motte to Miss Katharine Deas, Daughter of David Deas, Esq; deceased.—Lieut. William Moultrie to Miss Hannah Ainslie, Daughter of John Ainslie, Esq; deceased.—Hon. Henry Middleton, Esq; to the Hon. Lady Mary Ainslie, Widow of John Ainslie, Esq; deceased, and Daughter of the late Earl of Cromartie. (Friday, January 19, 1776.)

MARRIAGE. Isaac Macpherson, Esq; to Miss Sarah Perry, Daughter of Edward Perry, Esq; deceased. (Friday, February 9, 1776.)

MARRIAGES. William Gerard DeBrahm, Esq; to Mrs. Mary Fenwick, Widow of the late Hon. Edward Fenwicke, Esq; deceased—Lieutenant Benjamin Legaré to Miss Alice Cox, Daughter of the late Mr. George Cox, deceased; an amiable and accomplished young Lady. (Friday, March 8, 1776.)

MARRIAGE. Mr. Archer Smith, to Miss Florence Waring, Daughter of Benjamin Waring, Esq; deceased. (Wednesday, March 20, 1776.)

MARRIAGE. Mr. John Macpherson, to Miss Susannah Miles, Daughter of Silas Miles, Esq; deceased. (Wednesday, April 3, 1776.)

MARRIAGE. Capt. Charles Heatly to Miss Ann Sabb, Daughter of Mr. William Sabb, deceased. (Wednesday, April 10, 1776.)

MARRIAGES. Colonel Christopher Gadsden, to Miss Anne Wragg, Daughter of the Honourable Joseph Wragg, Esq; deceased.—Mr. William M'Gillvray, to Miss Anne Hinckley, Daughter of Mr. William Hinckley. (Wednesday, April 17, 1776.)

MARRIAGES. Lieut. George Mathewes to the amiable Miss Mary Saltus, Daughter of Richard Saltus, Esq; deceased—Capt. Edmund Richardson to Miss Rachel Heatley, Daughter of Capt. William Heatley of St. Matthew's Parish. (Wednesday, May 8, 1776.)

MARRIAGES. Mr. Henry Nicholes, to Miss Sarah Fuller, Daughter of Thomas Fuller, Esq;—Capt. Samuel Legaré, to Miss Eleanor Hoyland, Daughter of Mr. Thomas Hoyland, deceased; an accomplished young Lady, whose many amiable Endowments bid fair to ensure the Enjoyment of every Bliss attendant on the married State. (Wednesday, May 22, 1776.)

MARRIAGE. Mr. George Harland Hartley, to Miss Elisabeth Cuming. (Friday, August 2, 1776.)

MARRIAGES. Major James Mayson, to Miss Henrietta Hart, Daughter of the Rev. Mr. Samuel Hart.—Mr. William Bellamy to Mrs. Martha Baker, Widow of Doctor Richard Baker, deceased. (Wednesday, August 21, 1776.)

MARRIAGE. Capt. Roger Sanders, of the 1st Regiment, to the amiable Miss Amarinthia Lowndes, Daughter of the Hon. Rawlins Lowndes, Esq. (Wednesday, September 25, 1776.)

MARRIAGE. Lieut. Press Smith, to Miss Elisabeth Miles, Daughter of Silas Miles, Esq; deceased. (Wednesday, October 9, 1776.)

MARRIAGES. Mr. James Wier, to Mrs. Elisabeth Baird.—Mr. Patrick Moon, to Miss Martha Forrest. (Thursday, October 17, 1776.)

MARRIAGE. Mr. Peter Smith, to the amiable Miss Mary Middleton, Daughter of the Hon. Henry Middleton, Esq. (Thursday, November 21, 1776.)

MARRIAGE. Mr. John-Ernest Poyas, to Mrs. Mary Schwartzkorff, Widow of Dr. Schwartzkorff, deceased. (Thursday, November 28, 1776.)

MARRIAGE. Mr. Richard Wainwright, to the amiable Miss Anne Dewar, Daughter of Mr. Charles Dewar, deceased. (Thursday, December 12, 1776.)

MARRIAGE. Reverend Mr. Hill, to Mrs. Susanna Greene, Widow of Mr. Nathaniel Greene, deceased. (Thursday, December 19, 1776.)

MARRIAGES. William Mathewes, Esq; to Miss Elisabeth Coachman, Daughter of the deceased William Coachman, Esq.—Lieut. Peter Bounetheau, to Miss Elisabeth Weyman, Daughter of Mr. Edward Weyman.—Mr. Solomon Milner, to Miss Ann Ash, Daughter of the deceased Mr. Cato Ash.—Mr. John Abercrombie, to Mrs. Sarah Mitchell, Widow of the deceased Mr. Moses Mitchell. Mr. Peter Bottiton, to Mrs. Mary Air, Widow of the deceased Mr. William Air.—Mr. Matthias Hutchinson, to Mrs. Elisabeth Brandford, Widow of the deceased Mr. Barnet Brandford.—Mr. John Bennett, to Miss Mary Godfrey. (Thursday, January 16, 1777.)

MARRIAGE. Hopson Pinckney, Esq; to Miss Elisabeth Cannon, Daughter of Mr. Daniel Cannon. (Thursday, February 6, 1777.)

MARRIAGE. Solomon Freer, Esq; to Mrs. Ann Matthewes, Widow of the deceased Benjamin Matthewes, Esq. Mr. Elisha Sawyer, to the beautiful and accomplished Miss Ann Blake, Daughter of Edward Blake, Esq. (Thursday, February 13, 1777.)

MARRIAGE. Mr. M'Cartan Campbell, to Miss Sarah Fenwicke, Daughter of the Hon. Edward Fenwicke, Esq; deceased. (Thursday, February 27, 1777.)

MARRIAGE. Dr. Peter Fayssoux, to Mrs. Ann Johnston, Widow of the deceased William Johnston, Esq. (Thursday, March 20, 1777.)

MARRIAGES. Capt. John M'Call, to Miss Ann Lessesne, Daughter of the deceased Thomas Lessesne, Esq. Dr. James Air, to Miss Elisabeth Legaré, Daughter of Mr. Solomon Legaré, sen. (Thursday, April 10, 1777.)

MARRIAGE. Mr. James Touseger, to Miss Margaret Ball, Daughter of the deceased Mr. Samuel Ball. (Thursday, April 17, 1777.)

MARRIAGE. Mr. Robert Rivers, to Miss Ann Hanscome, Daughter of Mr. Thomas Hanscome. (Thursday, April 24, 1777.)

MARRIAGES. Capt. Joseph Glover, jun. to the amiable Mrs. Ann Webb, Widow of the late Benjamin Webb, Esq; deceased, a Lady possessed of every Accomplishment that can render the Married State happy.—Mr. John Bryan, Merchant, to Miss Rachel Simons, Daughter of the deceased Benjamin Simons, Esq. (Thursday, May 1, 1777.)

MARRIAGES. John Harleston, jun. Esq; to Miss Elisabeth Lynch, Daughter of the deceased Thomas Lynch, Esq.—Mr. Jonathan Lawrence, to Miss Sarah Daniel, Daughter of Robert Daniel, Esq.—Mr. James M'Call, to Miss Ann Dart, Daughter of the Hon. Benjamin Dart, Esq.—Mr. Edward Trescott, to Miss Katharine Bocquet, Daughter of Mr. Peter Bocquet.—Mr. William Wayne, to Miss Esther Trezevant, Daughter of the deceased Mr. Daniel Trezevant. (Thursday, May 8, 1777.)

MARRIAGES. John Barnwell, jun. Esq; to Miss Ann Hutson, Daughter of the Reverend Mr. William Hutson, deceased. Capt. Richard Cogdell, of the 5th Regiment, to Miss Mary Stevens, Daughter of the deceased Mr. John Stevens . (Thursday, May 15, 1777.)

MARRIAGES. Mr. Richard Cole, to Miss Ann Boomer, Daughter of Mr. Jacob Boomer.—Mr. Henry Byers, to Miss Catharine Delka, Daughter of Mr. John Delka. (Thursday, May 29, 1777.)

MARRIAGE. At Georgetown, Mr. John Wilson, to Miss Margaret Hazell, Daughter of the deceased Thomas Hazell, Esq. (Thursday, June 12, 1777.)

MARRIAGE. Mr. William Long, Merchant, to Mrs. Elisabeth Kirkwood, Widow of the deceased Mr. Alexander Kirkwood. (Thursday, June 26, 1777.)

MARRIAGES. Lieut. David Dubois, to Miss Susanna Muncreef, Daughter of Mr. Richard Muncreef.—Mr. John Saunders, to Mrs. Martha Hunt, Widow of the deceased Mr. Joseph Hunt, of Godfrey's Savannah.—Mr. David Douglass, to Miss Weatherford, Daughter of Martin Weatherford, Esq; of Augusta. (Thursday, July 10, 1777.)

MARRIAGES. Charles Dupont, Esq; to Miss Sarah Coachman, Daughter of Benjamin Coachman, Esq.—Mr. Thomas Hendlin, to Mrs. Amy Arnold, Widow of the deceased Mr. Thomas Arnold. (Thursday, July 17, 1777.)

MARRIAGE. Mr. George Cooke, Merchant, to Mrs. Eleanor Wade, Widow of the deceased Mr. Richard Wade. (Thursday, July 24, 1777.)

MARRIAGE. Dr. Francis-Walter Marshall, to Miss Mary Hinds, Daughter of Mr. Patrick Hinds. (Thursday, August 28, 1777.)

MARRIAGE. Charles Clifford, Esq; to Miss Elisabeth Perry, Daughter of the deceased Josiah Perry, Esq. (Thursday, September 11, 1777.)

MARRIAGES. Mr. Thomas Smith, to Miss Jane Young, Daughter of Mr. Thomas Young.—Capt. Thomas Chenie, to Miss Elisabeth Wood.—Mr. David Burger, to Miss Mary Nelmes. (Thursday, November 6, 1777.)

MARRIAGES. Benjamin Smith, jun. Esq; to Miss Sarah Dry, daughter of the Hon. William Dry, Esq.—Gabriel Capers, Esq; to Miss Sarah Lloyd, daughter of the deceased Mr. William Lloyd.—Mr. John Withers, to Miss Frances Gray, daughter of the deceased Henry Gray, Esq.—Capt. Abraham-Mendas Sexias, to Miss Ritsey Hart, daughter of Mr. Joshua Hart. (Thursday, November 20, 1777.)

MARRIAGE. Capt. John Blake to Miss Margaret Mercier, daughter of the deceased Capt. Peter Mercier. (Thursday, November 27, 1777.)

MARRIAGE. Mr. Thomas Cochran, to Mrs. Susanna Hawie, widow of the deceased Mr. Robert Hawie. (Thursday, December 25, 1777.)

MARRIAGE. Colonel Isaac Motte, of the 2d regiment, to Miss Mary Broughton, daughter of the deceased Alexander Broughton, Esq. (Thursday, January 1, 1778.)

MARRIAGES. William Heyward, Esq; to Miss Hannah Shubrick, daughter of the Hon. Thomas Shubrick, Esq.—Mr. Othniel Giles, to Lady Jane Colleton, widow of the deceased Sir John Colleton, Bart.—Mr. Joseph Moore, to Mrs. Anne Taylor, widow of the deceased Mr. John Taylor, Mr. Tobias Cambridge, to Miss Elisabeth Wood, daughter of the deceased Mr. William Wood. (Thursday, January 8, 1778.)

MARRIAGES. John Mowatt, Esq; to Miss Mary Ash, daughter of the deceased Mr. Cato Ash.—Mr. Paul Taylor, to Miss Martha Miller, daughter of Mr. William Miller.—Mr. Joseph Lafar, to Miss Catharine Boilliat, daughter of Mr. David Boilliat. (Thursday, January 29, 1778.)

MARRIAGES. Major Samuel Wise, to Mrs. Ann Beatty, widow of the deceased Mr. Francis Beatty.—William Taggart, Esq; to Mrs. Mary Haly, widow of the deceased Dr. John Haly. (Thursday, February 5, 1778.)

MARRIAGE. Mr. William Vaux, of Georgetown, to Miss Ann Pawley, daughter of Capt. Percival Pawley, of Waccamaw. (Thursday, February 12, 1778.)

MARRIAGES. Mr. Richard Perry, to Miss Helen Hunter, daughter of the deceased Mr. James Hunter. Mr. Albert-Aerney Muller, to Miss Magdalen Martin, daughter of the Rev. Mr. Nicholas Martin, pastor of the Lutheran church in Charlestown.—Mr. David-Frederick Cruger, to Miss Isabella Liston. (Thursday, February 19, 1778.)

MARRIAGE. Dr. Cornelius Dysart, to Miss Charity Jack, daughter of Mr. Patrick Jack of N. Carolina. (Thursday, February 26, 1778.)

MARRIAGE. Capt. Clement Conyers, to Miss Francis Snell. (Thursday, March 12, 1778.)

MARRIAGES. Mr. Andrew Dewees, to Miss Katharine Chicken, daughter of the deceased Mr. William Chicken. Mr. Thomas Withers, to Mrs. Deveaux, widow of the deceased Mr. Andrew Deveaux. (Thursday, March 19, 1778.)

MARRIAGE. Mr. Paul Walter, to Miss Ann Geigleman, daughter of the deceased Mr. Emanuel Geigleman. (Thursday, March 26, 1778.)

MARRIAGE. Mr. John Waring, jun. to Miss Ann Smith, daughter of Henry Smith, Esq; of Goosecreek. (Thursday, April 16, 1778.)

MARRIAGES. Mr. William Roach, to Miss Mary Campbell, of Christ Church Parish.—Mr. John Peak, to Miss Elizabeth Harvey. (Thursday, April 23, 1778.)

MARRIAGES. Capt. Thomas Shubrick, of the 5th regiment, to Miss Mary Brandford, daughter of the deceased ——— Brandford, Esq.—Mr. George Barksdale, of Christ Church Parish, to Miss Mary Daniel, daughter of the deceased John Daniel, Esq.—Mr. Richard Latham, to Miss Grace Forbes. (Thursday, April 30, 1778.)

MARRIAGES. Mr. Joseph Waring, to Miss Mary Joor, daughter of the deceased John Joor, Esq.—Mr. Thomas Waring, to Miss Martha Waring, daughter of the deceased Mr. Joseph Waring.—William Nisbett, Esq; to Miss Jane Scott.—Mr. Stolberg Adler, to Miss Ann Rodgaman.—Capt. John Evans, to Miss Mary Anderson. (Thursday, May 7, 1778.)

MARRIAGE. John Rose, Esq; to Miss Susannah I'on, daughter of the deceased Capt. George I'on. (Thursday, May 14, 1778.)

MARRIAGE. Mr. George Rout, to Mrs. Ann Parker, widow of the deceased Mr. George Parker, merchant. (Thursday, May 21, 1778.)

MARRIAGE. Mr. Jacob Valk, to Mrs. Ann Roberts, widow of the deceased Dr. William Roberts. (Thursday, May 28, 1778.)

MARRIAGE. Mr. John Splatt Cripps to Miss Elisabeth Farr, daughter of Thomas Farr, Esq. (Thursday, June 4, 1778.)

MARRIAGE. Mr. John Lessesne to Miss Mary Frederick, daughter of the deceased Mr. Jeremiah Frederick. (Thursday, July 9, 1778.)

MARRIAGE. Capt. Philip Sullivan, to Miss Susannah Shackleford, daughter of the deceased Mr. ——— Shackleford. (Thursday, July 16, 1778.)

MARRIAGES. Rev. Mr. Christian Streight, Pastor of the Lutheran, Church in this town, to Miss Mary Hoof—At St. Helena, Mr. John Dedier to Miss Margaret Cook. (Thursday, July 30, 1778.)

MARRIAGES. Mr. Thomas Rivers, to Miss Mary Warham, daughter of Mr. Charles Warham.—Capt. Cornelius Schermerhorn, to Miss Carolina Snyder, daughter of Mr. Paul Snyder.— Mr. Richard Woodcraft, to Miss Rizpah Rivers, daughter of the deceased Mr. John Rivers. (Thursday, September 3, 1778.)

MARRIAGE. Mr. Abraham Sasportas to Miss Rachael Da Costa, daughter of Mr. Isaac Da Costa. (Thursday, September 17, 1778.)

MARRIAGE. Mr. William Day to Miss Elizabeth Postell, daughter of the deceased James Postell, Esq; of Dorchester. (Thursday, September 24, 1778.)

MARRIAGE. Capt. James Ladson, of the 1st regiment, to Miss Judith Smith, daughter of the deceased Hon. Benjamin Smith, Esq. (Thursday, October 8, 1778.)

MARRIAGES. Capt. Thomas Gadsden, of the 1st Regiment, to Miss Martha Fenwicke daughter of the Hon. Edward Fenwicke, Esq; deceased—Mr. Andrew Hazell, to Miss Mary Milner, Daughter of the deceased Job Milner, Esq—At Williamsburgh, Virginia, St. George Tucker, Esq; of the Island of Bermuda, to Mrs. Randolph, Matoax, in Prince George. (Thursday, October 15, 1778.)

MARRIAGE. Mr. Thomas Elfe to Miss Mary Pagett. (Thursday, November 5, 1778.)

MARRIAGES. Andrew Leitch, Esq; to Mrs. Catharine Spooler, widow of the deceased Mr. George Spooler.—Mr. John Holmes, to Miss Helen Boomer, daughter of Mr. John Boomer.—Mr. John Stokes, to Miss Margaret Young, daughter of Mr. Thomas Young. (Thursday, November 12, 1778.)

MARRIAGE. Dr. Oliver Hart to Miss Sarah Brockington. (Thursday, November 19, 1778.)

MARRIAGES. Capt. Benjamin Mathews to Miss Mary Mathews, daughter of the deceased William Mathews, Esq; Mr. James Edwards to Miss Rebecca Fripp, daughter of Capt. John Fripp, of St. Helena. (Thursday, November 26, 1778.)

MARRIAGE. Mr. Alexander Rantowle to Miss Eleanor Wardrobe. (Thursday, December 3, 1778.)

MARRIAGE. Mr. Richard Muncreef, to Miss Elisabeth Young, daughter of the deceased Major William Young.—Thomas Middleton, Esq; of Crowfield, to Miss Elizabeth Deas, daughter of the deceased David Deas, Esq.—Mr. Samuel Mordecai, to Miss Catharine Andrews, daughter of Mr. Abraham Andrews. (Thursday, December 24, 1778.)

MARRIAGES. William Scott, jun. Esq; to Miss Elisabeth Rivers, daughter of the deceased Mr. Jonathan Rivers. Capt. Benjamin Tucker, to Miss Sarah Ballantine, daughter of the deceased Mr. ——— Ballantine.—Mr. William Trusler, to Miss Jane Anderson, daughter of the deceased Mr. Hugh Anderson.—Capt. Alexander Boyce, of the 6th regiment, to Mrs. Catharine-Othelia M'Allister, widow of the deceased Capt. M'Allister. (Thursday, December 31, 1778.)

MARRIAGE. Alexander Rose, Esq; to Miss Margaret Smith, daughter of the Hon. William Smith Esq; deceased, late Chief Justice of New York.—Mr. Francis Bonneau, to Miss Hannah Elfe, daughter of deceased Mr. Thomas Elfe. (Thursday, January 21, 1779.)

MARRIAGES. Mr. Jeremiah Rose to Miss Susanna Stent—Mr. John Singleton to Miss Jane Miller. (Thursday, March 18, 1779.)

MARRIAGES. Mr. Stephen Baker, son of Col. John Baker, late of Georgia, to Mrs. Martha Fuller, daughter of William Fuller, Esq; deceased.—Capt. William Ransom Davis, of the 5th regiment, to Miss Eleanore Norville.—Mr. David Stevens, to Mrs. Mary Adams.—Andrew Quelch, Esq; to Mrs. Sarah Fyffe, widow of the deceased Mr. John Fyffe.—Mr. Thomas Tims, to Miss Anne Hext. (Friday, April 23, 1779.)

MARRIAGE. Capt. Benjamin Stone to Miss Lovey Rivers, daughter of Col. Robert Rivers. (Friday, July 30, 1779.)

MARRIAGES. Mr. Edmund Petrie to Miss Anne Peronneau, daughter of the deceased Alexander Peronneau, Esq;—William Bull jun. Esq; to Miss Elizabeth Reid, daughter of the deceased Dr. Reid—Mr. Gershon Cohen, to Miss Rebecca Sarzidas, daughter of the deceased Mr. Abraham Sarzidas, of Georgia. (Friday, August 27, 1779.)

MARRIAGE. Mr. John Farr, to Mrs. Smith, widow of Mr. Press Smith, deceased. (Friday, September 24, 1779.)

MARRIAGES. Capt. John Wilson to Mrs. Mary Ladson, relict of Capt. Thomas Ladson, deceased—Daniel Tucker, Esq; of Georgetown to Miss Elizabeth Hyrne, Daughter of the late Col. Henry Hyrne. (Friday, October 1, 1779.)

MARRIAGE. Brigadier-General Moultrie to Mrs. Hannah Lynch, widow of the Honourable Thomas Lynch, Esq; deceased. (Friday, October 15, 1779.)

MARRIAGE. Mr. John David Miller, to Miss Jane Richton, daughter of Mr. M'Cully Righton. (Friday, October 29, 1779.)

MARRIAGE. Thomas Broughton, Esq; to Miss Susannah Donnom, daughter of the deceased James Donnom, Esq. (Friday, November 19, 1779.)

MARRIAGE. Mr. Edgar Wells, to Miss Claudia Bennett, daughter of the deceased Mr. —— Bennett. (Friday, December 3, 1779.)

MARRIAGE. Capt. Alexander Keith, to Miss Susannah Bullein, daughter of the deceased John Bullein, Esq. (Friday, December 10, 1779.)

MARRIAGES. Capt. John Hatter, to Mrs. Elisabeth Torrans, widow of the deceased Mr. John Torrans.—Ensign Robert Campbell, of the 71st regiment, to Miss Elisabeth Mitchell, daughter of Mr. John Mitchell. (Wednesday, November 1, 1780.)

MARRIAGE. Lieut. ARCHIBALD CAMPBELL, of the 71st regiment, to Miss MARGARET PHILP, daughter of Robert Philp, Esq. (Wednesday, December 20, 1780.)

MARRIAGES. Mr. Josiah Bonneau, to Miss Jean Bolton, daughter of the deceased Mr. James Bolton. (Wednesday, January 17, 1781.)

MARRIAGE. ROBERT M'CULLOH, Esq; to Miss ANNE ROUPELL, daughter of George Roupell, Esq; his Majesty's Post-Master General in the Southern District of North-America. (Wednesday, January 24, 1781.)

MARRIAGES. James Murray, Esq; of the Royal Navy, to Miss Elisabeth Elliott, daughter of the deceased Mr. Richard-Burnham Elliott.—Mr. John Smith, to Miss Ann White. (Saturday, February 24, 1781.)

MARRIAGE. Mr. Daniel Jenkins of Edisto, to Miss Martha Seabrook, daughter of the deceased Mr. Benjamin Seabrook. (Wednesday, February 28, 1781.)

THE ROYAL GAZETTE

MARRIAGES. Mr. John Glaze, of Dorchester, to Miss Joanna Dawson, daughter of Mr. John Dawson.—Mr. Job Colcock, to Miss Harriet Bradwell, daughter of the deceased Mr. Joseph Bradwell. (Wednesday, March 14, 1781.)

MARRIAGE. Last Thursday evening, Major JOHN CARDEN, of the Prince of Wales's American Regiment, to Miss JUDITH WRAGG, daughter of the Honourable William Wragg, Esq; deceased. (Saturday, March 17, 1781.)

MARRIAGE. Lieut. MACNEILL, of the 9th regiment, to Miss BLAIR SPENCE. (Wednesday, March 21, 1781.)

MARRIAGES. Mr. WILLIAM M'LEOD, to Miss MARY ALEXANDER, daughter of Mr. William Alexander.—Mr. GLEN. DRAYTON, to Miss ELISABETH ELLIOTT, daughter of the deceased Mr. Samuel Elliott.—Mr. JOHN KEMMELL, to Miss RACHEL LONG, daughter of Mr. Felix Long. (Wednesday, May 30, 1781.)

MARRIAGE. Mr. JOHN PARKINSON, to Miss KATHARINE NICHOLSON, daughter of the deceased Mr. Francis Nicholson. (Wednesday, July 11, 1781.)

MARRIAGE. Mr. JOHN CHAMPNEYS, to Mrs. MARY WILSON, Widow of the deceased Mr. William Wilson. (Wednesday, August 22, 1781.)

MARRIAGES. Capt. WIGHTMAN, of the Prince of Wales's American Regiment, to Miss SARAH BROWN, of Georgetown. Mr. STEPHEN BROWN, to Mrs. ELISABETH TALLMAN, widow of the deceased Mr. John-Richard Tallman.—Mr. ROBERT VARDELL, to Miss MARY WESTON. (Saturday, September 22, 1781.)

MARRIAGE. Mr. CHARLES FREER, to Miss MARY STANYARNE, daughter of Mr. William Stanyarne, of John's-Island. (Saturday, October 6, 1781.)

MARRIAGE. Mr. JOHN TUNNO, to Miss MARGARET ROSE, daughter of John Rose, Esq. (Saturday, October 20, 1781.)

MARRIAGE. Major JOHN COFFIN, of the Provincial Cavalry, to Miss ANNE MATHEWES, daughter of the deceased William Mathewes, Esq; of John's Island. (Wednesday, October 24, 1781.)

MARRIAGE. Capt. Roworth, of the King's Rangers, to Miss NANCY DEVEAUX, daughter of William Deveaux, Esq; of Beaufort, South Carolina. (Ibid.)

MARRIAGE. Mr. THOMAS ROPER, to Miss LYDIA HARVEY.—Mr. WILLIAM DEWEES, to MISS JANE ROGERS. (Saturday, November 10, 1781.)

MARRIAGE. Mr. RICHARD WRINCH, to Mrs. SARAH MACKENZIE, widow of the deceased Capt. Mackenzie. (Wednesday, November 14, 1781.)

MARRIAGE. Mr. RALPH DAWES, to Miss MARGARET PERONNEAU, daughter of the deceased Mr. Alexander Peronneau. (Saturday, November 17, 1781.)

On the 19th instant was married, at Beaufort, Major JOHN CARDEN, of the Prince of Wale's American Regiment, to Miss KITTY HAZARD, daughter of William Hazard, Esq; of that place. (Wednesday, November 28, 1781.)

MARRIAGE. Capt. GEORGE KER, of the 1st Battalion of General Delancey's Brigade, to Miss MARY FOTHERINGHAM, daughter of the late Dr. Alex. Fotheringham, of Dorchester. (Wednesday, December 5, 1781.)

MARRIAGE. Mr. ALEXANDER OLIPHANT, to MISS ELISABETH HAM, daughter of Mr. Thomas Ham. (Wednesday, December 12, 1781.)

MARRIAGE. Captain NORMAN M'LEOD, of the Provincial Light-Infantry, to Miss KATHARINE CAMPBELL, daughter of Alexander Campbell, Esq; of Balole, North-Britain; an amiable young Lady.

—Mr. NICOL PRIMEROSE, Merchant, to Miss KATHARINE LIVIE, daughter of the late Alexander Livie, Esquire. (Wednesday, March 13, 1782.)

MARRIAGE. Major GIBBS of the Royal Ninety-Six Militia to Mrs. JANE DOWNS widow of the deceased Major Downs, of the Royal Camden Militia. (Saturday, June 8, 1782.)

INDEX

Long, Rachel, 35.
Long, William, 27.
Lord, Andrew, 16.
Lord, John, 8.
Lowndes, Amarinthia, 25.
Lowndes, Rawlins, 25.
Lushington, Richard, 20.
Lutheran Church, Charles Town, 29, 31.
Lynch, Elizabeth, 27.
Lynch, Mrs. Hannah (Motte), 33.
Lynch, Sabina, 8.
Lynch, Thomas, 8, 27, 33.
MacGaw, Sally, 17.
Mackay, John, 12.
Mackay, Polly, 12.
Mackay, Robert, 18.
Mackenzie, Captain, 36.
Mackenzie, Anne, 19.
Mackenzie, John, 12.
Mackenzie, Mary, 15.
Mackenzie, Mrs. Sarah, 36.
Mackenzie, Robert, 15.
Mackenzie, William, 19.
MacNeill, Lieutenant, 35.
MacNeill, Dr. Archibald, 13, 23.
MacNeill, Mrs. Margaret, 23.
Macpherson, Isaac, 24.
Macpherson, John, 24.
Macpherson, Ulysses, 15.
Mann, Dr., 12.
Mann, Sukey, 12 (erroneously given Nancy).
Marchant, Benjamin, 11.
Marshall, Dr. Francis Walter, 28.
Martin, H. M. S., 14.
Martin, Mrs. Elizabeth, 20.
Martin, John, 20.
Martin, Magdalen, 29.
Martin, Rev. Nicholas, 29.
Mathewes, Anne, 13 ("Nancy").
Mathewes, Anne (later), 36.
Mathewes, Mrs. Ann, 26.
Mathewes, Benjamin, 14, 26.
Mathewes, Benjamin (later), 32.
Mathewes, Mrs. Charlotte, 12.
Mathewes, George, 24.
Mathewes, James, 12.
Mathewes, John, 13.
Mathewes, John, son of James, 8.

Mathewes, John (changed the spelling of his name to Mathews), son of John, 7.
Mathewes, John Raven, 23.
Mathewes, Mary, 32.
Mathewes, Susannah, 22.
Mathewes, William, 22, 32, 36.
Mtahewes, William (later), 26.
Matoax (Virginia), 31.
Maverick, Samuel, 19.
Mayson, James, 25.
Mazÿck, Alexander, 16.
Mazÿck, Isaac, 22.
Mazÿck, Mary Ann, 22.
Mazÿck, Paul, 22.
McAllister, Captain, 32.
McAllister, Mrs. Catharine Othelia, 32.
McCall, James, 27.
McCall, John, Jr., 10, 26.
McCulloh, Robert, 34.
McGillivray, William, 24.
McKewn, Robert, 13, 19.
McKewn, Sarah Elliott, 19.
McKewn, Susannah, 13.
McLeod, Norman, 36.
McLeod, William, 35.
McQueen, John, 8.
McQueen, Nancy, 8.
Mellichamp, Martha, 19.
Mercier, Margaret, 28.
Mercier, Peter, 28.
Michie, Alexander, 7.
Middleton, Henry, 24, 25.
Middleton, Mary, daughter of Thomas, 16 ("Polly").
Middleton, Mary, daughter of Henry, 25.
Middleton, Sarah, 7.
Middleton, Thomas (1719-1766), 7, 16.
Middleton, Thomas (175.-1779), 21.
Middleton, Thomas (cousin), 32.
Miles, Acquilla, 18.
Miles, Edward, 7.
Miles, Elizabeth, 25.
Miles, Mrs. Elizabeth, 7.
Miles, Mrs. Mary, 22.
Miles, Patty, 10.
Miles, Silas, 24, 25.